Insight into Traditional, Hybrid & Self Publishing

STEPS TO PUBLISHING:

WHAT YOU NEED TO KNOW

JUDY RANKIN

Published by Jaymah
Cover Art by Judy Rankin

ISBN: 978-0-6453770-8-8

"I've written the manuscript, now what?"

The options for publishing are extensive. The main that comes to mind is a traditional publishing house. With technological advances, writers are not limited to traditional publishing. What about self-Publishing and hybrid publishing? Despite what the popular view may be, there is no right or wrong option. No matter what option you choose, it's important to be informed and understand each of the options available to you.

Formatting for Print
Scribus

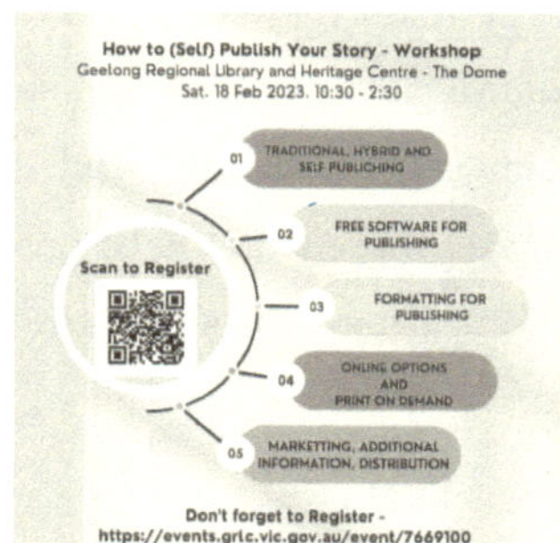
How to (Self) Publish Your Story - Workshop
Geelong Regional Library and Heritage Centre - The Dome
Sat. 18 Feb 2023. 10:30 - 2:30
Scan to Register
01 TRADITIONAL, HYBRID AND SELF PUBLISHING
02 FREE SOFTWARE FOR PUBLISHING
03 FORMATTING FOR PUBLISHING
04 ONLINE OPTIONS AND PRINT ON DEMAND
05 MARKETTING, ADDITIONAL INFORMATION, DISTRIBUTION
Don't forget to Register -
https://events.grlc.vic.gov.au/event/7669100

"GET YOUR STORY OFF YOUR COMPUTER AND INTO THE WORLD"
SOLD OUT!
HOW TO (SELF) PUBLISH YOUR STORY
WITH JUDY RANKIN
18 FEB 2023 / 10:30 - 2:30
Geelong Regional Library and Heritage Centre - The Dome

Praise for Workshops

Geelong Regional Library

February 2022

'I didn't realise there were so many options'

P.J.

'I was suprised by the amount of information Judy gave us!'

M.P.

Southern Grampians Library

September 2024

'Very engaging'

N.T.

'Great resources and *lots* of information. Thank you.'

E.G.

CONTENTS

Who Am I?

As the saying goes, there's more than one way to skin a cat. And there's more than one way to publish a story. My publishing knowledge was learned out of necessity. I fell in love with creative writing in Grade 4 when my teacher, Mr Cox, read Charlotte's Web to the class. I decided there and then that I would write stories when I grew up—either that or drive a tram! But that's another story.

The next 30+ years were spent saying, 'One day, I'll write a book.' When my 39-year-old sister was diagnosed with a life-threatening illness, the harsh reality that tomorrow wasn't promised pushed me to stop saying 'one day' and start writing. And what better way to start than to coerce three family members into telling a story about my sister? The manuscript It's [Not] All About Liz! [INAAL] was pitched to publishers and ended on many slush piles. The search for a publisher wasn't limited to Australia, as an illness narrative has a global resonance. Working with a US publisher, their editor wanted to take out our Australianisms to make it easier for US readers to understand. This defeated the purpose, as far as I could see. I didn't want just to publish a story; I wanted to publish our story and we speak Australian. Eventually, the book was published through a hybrid publisher, Balboa Press [USA], in 2014. It was a conscious decision to pay a publisher as it allowed us to keep the integrity of the story we wanted to tell while having a professional publish and distribute it through their networks—something I didn't (yet) know how to do.

The experience was generally a positive one. While it cost me around $4,000, I was happy with the result and coverage. However, the return on my investment was low, which made me consider future publications. I didn't want to be forking out thousands of dollars I didn't have each time I wrote a book only to make a minimal financial return.

Around this time, I signed up for a ten-week short course on scriptwriting through RMIT in Melbourne to better understand what was involved. I thought INAAL would make a great movie, but I needed to learn what that entailed. This ten-week course was the best thing I'd ever done. I loved it! Learning about beats and acts and sequences enthralled me. Discovering the technical side of scriptwriting made me want to know more about the technical side of fiction and nonfiction writing.

To cut a long story short, I enrolled in a Professional Writing and Publishing degree, followed by an Honours year, followed by a PhD, all the while continuing to work on the craft of writing.

My next novel, Catelina, was published through a UK publisher. While the publisher was a smaller traditional company, the three-year contract left a bitter taste in my mouth. What I saw as a way forward for the manuscript differed from the publisher. I wanted to explore foreign rights, but the publisher didn't. I saw opportunities for public exposure, but the publisher said no. It was frustrating as I didn't understand what was happening. So, I continued to research and learn about the publishing industry.

I began to notice a trend. It seemed you either needed to be famous to be noticed by the big traditional publishers (I wasn't) or have thousands of dollars (I didn't) to pay someone to publish your work. Entrusting your work to a traditional publisher also came with the loss of control. It was annoying that everything came with a cost—financial or other.

While pursuing university studies, I sold a few short stories to magazines, wrote several more manuscripts and advanced my education. With an honours degree in Professional Writing and Publishing and ten years of researching the publishing industry, I want to share with other writers what I've learned. I want to give away the trade secrets—or the ones I knew—so others can save time and money. There is no right or wrong to publishing. It will depend on the writer's goals. However, a writer needs to know what options there are, how to achieve them, and what industry expectations are.

In this book, I share my experiences as well as things to consider before getting or trying to get published. In many ways, writing a manuscript is the easy part. There are so many more factors to take into consideration. I'll tackle some of these in the following pages to get you thinking. This is not a definitive guide or process. It's a book with information to help you decide what path you'd like to take and what you need to know to get there. The focus is on giving you resources to take control of your work—whether through traditional, self or hybrid publishing. What I want you to take away from this book applies whether you're approaching a publishing house or self-publishing. While I will refer to books and novels, I'm not limiting this to these formats. It may be comics, graphic novels, ebooks, physical books, or any public production of your private work.

Getting published and selling stories is not easy. Don't be put off by the hurdles ahead. Find a community of like-minded people to bounce off, give you strength when you're pulling your hair out and share ideas.

Good luck!

Published Works by Judy Rankin

NOVELS

It's [Not] All About Liz! (2014) Balboa Press, USA
Catelina (2017) Pegasus, UK
The Land of Giant Pineapples (2022) Jaymah
Gilderoy (2024) by Sage Quinn, Jaymah
Short Stories by Judy Rankin (2025) Jaymah
Steps to Publishing: What You Need to Know (2025) Jaymah

ANTHOLOGIES

Short stories published in Geelong Writers Anthologies 2021, 2022, 2024
Coffee House Writers (2023)
online magazine (publishing fortnightly short stories)

FEATURE ARTICLES

'Baverstock Graves: For King and Country' (2015)
MUFTI RSL Victoria magazine
'Forty Year Crush' (2019)
that's life! Mega Monthly magazine

About the Author

Judy Rankin has been writing and journaling for as long as she can remember! However, in 2014, her writing became public after the release of her first book. Since her debut, Judy has released several novels, published in various magazines, anthologies, and journals. Torquay is home where she lives with her husband. She is currently completing a creative-practice PhD in Media and Communication. When not writing stories or studying, Judy has her finger in many pies—one offering services as a publishing consultant. She holds interactive workshops covering topics such as How to (Self) Publish Your Story and Creative Writing: the Story Behind the Story. She is an active member of Geelong Writers and believes telling stories is an integral part of life.

Judy enjoys writing less restrictive short stories, middle-grade readers, and even romance. However, much of her writing falls into the nonfiction/creative nonfiction genre. While open to experimenting in different genres, stories with a deeper meaning beyond the apparent story are always more appealing to write. It may be a theme or subject matter that has meaning to provoke conversation, thought and reflection about our Western or Australian society.

ACTIVITY ONE: Who Am I?

This book is a resource with information on the publishing industry. The chapters can be read consecutively or chosen randomly as a standalone chapter. If you're just starting to look at publishing, I'd suggest reading consecutively from chapter one to get a good overview of the process.

Throughout this book, activities will help to build a better understanding of yourself as a writer and where you want to go. While the activities may seem a little random, by the end of the book, you will have all the information you need to create an author bio and/or resume —a must if you are to 'sell' yourself as a writer.

What better way to start a book than to start with a question? Who Are You? You need to consider this question if you want to be a published writer. It is also one of the most challenging questions to answer. Writing an author bio and speaking about yourself is tough. It's more than your name or pseudonym.

Many think writing a story (whether a novel, short story or feature article) is about putting the words on a page. However, that's just one step. Once the words are on the page, you must 'sell' the idea to others. That means being able to tell others who you are, what you do and why you do it.

The aim is to start broad and refine who you are as a writer and where you are going. Answer the questions and don't worry too much if you're unsure. That's what we hope to hone in on as we go.

Let's get started!

•Name ____

• Describe who you are. Editor, dreamer, creative, wannabe.

____

____

____

• What stage are you at?

____

____

____

• What do you want to achieve?

____

____

____

• Who is your (reader) audience? Age, genre, male/female, etc.

____

____

____

Example 2

• Name: Jessie McGregor

• Describe who you are: Dreamer/Writer

• What stage are you at? Draft manuscript complete

• What do you want to achieve? To publish my book

• Who is your (reader) audience? Anyone aged 18+ who likes crime

We'll revisit this activity later in the book.

Elements of Production

Editing all sorts

You've got your completed manuscript (MS). You're happy with it. You've read it a few times and made some corrections or alterations. Maybe you've run it through software like Grammarly or ProWriter to improve it. Are you ready to send it out into the world? Nope. If you haven't, you need to edit your work – better still, have someone else edit your work.

The term 'editing' is an all-encompassing term. But what does it refer to? Well, that depends. There is developmental editing, structural editing, substantive, global, comprehensive, copy, big suggestion, closer detail editing... The list goes on.

Being the writer, you can be too close to see what fresh eyes pick up in your MS. What we think we're saying and how it comes out can be two different things. For example, you can see in your mind's eye what a character looks like, how they speak, their strengths and weaknesses, but this may not be conveyed in your writing.

Editing to consider before publishing

While editing is crucial to ensuring your manuscript is up to scratch, some edits need to be highlighted.

If you start to twitch as soon as you hear the word' editor,' you can be forgiven. Unfortunately, it is a necessary evil (editors aren't evil, but the editing process can be excruciating at times.). Yes, an editor can cause money to start flying out the window, but there are things you can do yourself before engaging a paid editor.

When I edit, I will conduct one edit at a time. For example, for the first read-through, I may look at grammar and spelling. Second read, I may look at organisation. The number of read-throughs and edits will vary, but with each one, I am focusing on a different element. Trying to do them all in one read-through is almost impossible.

Here is a brief explanation of what I would argue are the primary editing considerations needed - and you can do yourself - before showing your manuscript to anyone else. (And, yes, you need to show your MS to others before publishing. But I'll get to that later.) The list is general and is meant to give a broad overview. Appendix A includes websites and software that can help with some of these processes. Some are free to use; others may cost money.

Copy Editing

Copy editing is the mechanics of the writing. It is the technical stuff. The four components—or the Four Cs—when executed correctly, enhance the overall objective of communication. They are:

Clarity - Can the reader understand what you have written? Does it make sense? Or can it be misconstrued, pulling the reader out of the story? This might be through sentence structure or ambiguity.

Consistency - Consistency illustrates the connection and order between the components of the story. Here's an example of this. A character knocks on a door and opens it before entering a room, only to find that the door is shut three pages later and the character is still outside. In another example (from a book I read recently by a well-known author and publishing house), the character was clothed casually in shorts and a t-shirt - only to then read several pages later that she wore long pants and a shirt. As the reader, it was enough for me to stop reading and backtrack several pages, thinking I'd missed something. I hadn't. No one picked up on this consistency issue.

Coherence - how our sentences and paragraphs come together to tell the story. This can include the length of a sentence. Short, punchy sentences convey this better than long, drawn-out sentences if a situation is intense. Look at what is linking sentences or paragraphs. Do the links move smoothly? Or do you lose the essence of meaning because the structure is clunky?

Correctness - This is good old-fashioned spelling and grammar. I don't think I need to explain this too much. If you're a writer, you know there are spelling and grammar rules to follow. If spelling and grammar aren't your strong suit, invest in an editing and/or style manual.

Another thing to consider when writing in English is choosing what type of English to use: UK, Australian, American... This may change depending on the location of your audience. For example, you live in Australia but write articles for a US magazine. They will expect you to write in American English. It doesn't matter as much if you're writing a novel, but make sure you stick to it, whichever you choose. If you swap between spelling 'colour' with a 'u' in one chapter and without it in another, this shows a lack of professionalism that could cost you a book deal with a Big 5 publisher. It may also disrupt the reader, pulling them out of the story. We want them to stay in the story without interruption.

In Order of Importance

Correctness - get the mechanics of grammar and spelling as close to perfect as possible. There are several books worth looking at if you want to be precise with Australian grammar and style. They are Style Manual ISBN 9-780701-636487 and The Australian Editing Handbook ISBN 9-781118-635957.

Consistency – the correlating parts need to line up. Another way to put it is don't cut up the carrots before they've been harvested.

Clarity - check your language. The types of words and number of syllables in a children's book will differ greatly from those written for academia.

Coherence - does it flow?

Developmental Editing

While copy editing focuses on the mechanics of writing, developmental editing—also known as structural editing—focuses on the meaning and content. It's looking at the big picture of story elements. As a writer, you can see exactly how the story develops and what one thing means in relation to another. However, that may not always come through in the writing. Developmental edition allows an outsider's perspective of how the story is coming across. This might include the theme/subject matter, organisation, plot, pace, characterisation, dialogue, style, tone and sensitivity.

Here are some things to consider.

Organisation - This looks at the order in which things happen. That doesn't mean the story has to be linear or chronological. The story can jump around as much as you like! However, it still needs to be organised. Think about the sequences; how does one sequence interact with another? Think about descriptions; are they consistent? Think about cause and effect, compare and contrast, problems and solutions. Are things happening that don't move the story forward?

Plot - This can be a tricky one. Many writers don't plot out their stories before sitting down to write. They start creating and see where inspiration takes them. Others (myself included) are 'architects'. They plot out the whole novel before writing a word. Either way is fine, but the plot is what happens in the story and the points that need to be organised. How is Section 1 related to and linked with section 2? Is it plausible? Even futuristic and vampire stories need to be plausible. Plotting is a series of events that move the story forward. Plot and organise well and your futuristic vampire won't leave your readers screwing up their face in disbelief.

Pace - The speed of your story is something to monitor. You need exciting highs and calm lows. Readers will be exhausted if it's go, go, go all the way through. Alternatively, they may give up on the story if there's not enough action. So, the pace needs to be balanced. A good way to think about it is in terms of Action/Reaction. How many Action and Reaction sections you write will differ depending on who taught you to write, or where you get your information from. Just keep pace in mind as you read through your manuscript.

Characterisation - This is looking at your characters. What do they look like? What's their personality? Are they believable? Are they consistent? This is another one that can bring writers undone. As you write, you can see the character. You know them well! But ask yourself, will the reader see what you see? The characterisation can be revealed slowly as the story progresses, but you should leave no doubt in the reader's mind who or what this character is.

Dialogue - As the word suggests, it's what characters say. However, it's not just what they say; it's how they say it. If you are a middle-aged woman and your character is a 12-year-old boy living in London's East End, it's highly unlikely he'll speak as you do. He may talk using Cockney slang (apples and pears = stairs), drop the 'h' at the beginnings of words ('opefully), pronounce 'f' instead of 'th' ('fink' instead of 'think'), etc. Get into your character and know their tone of voice and speech style.

Style-Language and Tone - This element, while similar to the previous, goes a step further to the overall style and tone of the novel. If you're writing a historical novel set in outback Australia, you want the style and tone to reflect the period and characters of the time. If you're writing a romantic comedy, is your tone light and comedic? What's the tone of the narrator or POV (point of view) character? Is it consistent with the setting and period?

Sensitivity - This is a more recent concept that you may or may not take into consideration. Some may see it as political correctness, but it's more than that. It's about sensitivity around representing cultures or groupings other than your own. For example, having a character that is a Zulu warrior when you are of British decent, live in New Zealand and have never had contact with Africans, let alone Zulus warriors. There's no reason why you can't have a Zulu warrior as a character, but think about how you are presenting them. What are you basing your knowledge on? How would someone from the Zulu nation feel about this presentation? If you don't know, then maybe you need to ask one.

There is an ongoing debate around representation. You can buy into the discussion or ignore it. It's up to you. However, I'd err on the side of caution. You don't want to find yourself embroiled in negative backlash because something you wrote has been taken the wrong way. (I don't subscribe to, there's no such thing as 'bad' publicity. There is and it can hurt debut novelists.) Getting feedback from someone from the culture or group you are writing about doesn't take much. Find a sensitivity reader. Google will help you find them.

Proofreading

When proofreading, there are specific things you want to check and you will need to proofread several times after each edit to check corrections. You will proofread your manuscript before sending it out for editing to ensure you're sending a clean document. And before you submit it to a publisher, ensure you have adhered to their submission guidelines (e.g., font style and size, line spacing, word count, etc.). If self-publishing, you'll proofread the printer's copy before going into full publication (this is one step before ordering the 'proof' copy).

It sounds like a lot of reading, and it is. But in my experience, different formats will highlight different potential errors. While all of the writing and editing may happen on a computer screen, I see things in the print version that I don't notice on the screen.

Similarly, when the proof copy of the book arrives (and the end is in sight!), I read it as I would any other novel. Any last-minute changes that are needed. This also becomes a visual edit. How do the words look on the page? The thing I'm looking for is pages with a correct typeset.

That is:

• margins - the white space around the edge of the page is uniform and as per book size for print

• widows, orphans and runts – a single word at the end of a paragraph on a line by itself, or one line of text that sits all by itself at the beginning or end of a page (see examples on page 59 – Appendix B)

• paragraph identification and alignment

• rivers - when looking at a page, you may notice obvious white space running between words. There is always white space between words, but this looks a little more pronounced and can distract the reader (see examples on page 59 – Appendix B)

• section breaks - a chapter may start in the morning and move to an event later in the day. This may be shown on a page as a double space, character or symbol between paragraphs where the morning ends and the later events begin.

• word spacing - ensure there is no more than one space between words.

• letter spacing - ensure words don't appear w ith spaces wh ere the y shouldn't be.

• end-of-line breaks - generally automatic when typed on a computer. Preferably keeping words whole, not spl-

iced onto the next line.

• typeface/font - consistent through text, but may include things like foreign words spelled in italics, a long quote indented on both sides, etc.

• running headers/footers - are consistent.

Permissions

Permission covers some of the legal stuff surrounding copyright. I'm not going to say too much about copyright as I am not a lawyer. However, I know enough to know I cannot use someone else's image, drawing, words, etc, without permission. There are, of course, exemptions to this. For example, things in what's called the 'public domain'. If you download a free image from the internet, you can use it without permission, even though you may not know who created the image.

If you want to quote someone, this may be allowed (depends on your project, the length of the quote, if the quote is out of copyright - i.e. 70 years in Australia). I would advocate referencing somewhere in your book where the quote, image or concept came from if it is not your own. This applies to using images that you may have taken of people. You own the rights to the photo, but the person in the photo owns the rights to whether they want to be included in your picture.

You may be writing a fictional story but are using a real person or situation as a vehicle in the story. Do you have permission to tell their story? For example, I wrote a fictitious short story based on a private conversation. Names were changed and locations altered to protect the non-fictitious people. However, when my brother, who knew the story, read it online, he was horrified. I broke people's trust when I (stupidly) turned the situation into a fictitious story. I did not have permission to share what I did—even with a thin disguised.

Any time you publicly write about another person, make sure you've let them know and they're okay with it. Better still, ask them to sign a release form giving you permission to tell a story.

The general rule that I tell writers is if you are unsure if you have permission, find out. Ask Aunt Mary if she's happy for you to publish the picture you took of her at last year's family Christmas dinner. Google whether Shakespeare is still under copyright. Or speak to a lawyer. You don't want to be sued for plagiarism, stealing or using without permission.

A Final Word on Editors

If I'm asking someone else to edit my work, I want to make sure they are a subject expert and understand what readers what. If you are an editor, you want to improve the author, not just the manuscript. You are a bit like the reader's advocate.

Think about developmental editing as comprising two tasks that happen sequentially:

1/ Identify what works and what doesn't. How can it be improved?

2/ Figure out how best to communicate this to the author.

The editing process can take as long as the writing process. It shouldn't be rushed, as one slip-up may be the difference between a publisher taking you on or not. Your work is a reflection of you! Make sure you present well.

ACTIVITY TWO: Who Is Your Reader?

In this activity, I want to look at identifying your reading audience. It can sound easy; however, take some time to hone in on who really is your reader. Whether you realise it or not, what you have written will not appeal to everyone (sorry). While anyone can read your book, it's written (most likely) for a genre and specific audience. Being able to identify your reading audience enhances your appears as a professional and will help when it comes to marketing.

Think about the following:

1/ Gender: ______________________________

2/ Age: ______________________________

3/ Socio economic group: ______________________________

4/ Level of education: ______________________________

5/ Income (disposable or limited): ______________________________

6/ Demography: ______________________________

7/ Interests: ______________________________

8/Other genres they read: ______________________________

BE SPECIFIC! That way, you can target your audience better. Men and women think differently, as do adults and children.

Testing the Waters

You've finished your manuscript. You're pretty happy with it. It's been edited and it's time to go to print. Right? Not quite. It is time to start showing your baby to the world. Don't go to book print just yet. As I said before, we can't see our blind spots. It's better to test the waters, see how others respond, make adjustments if needed (I'd all but guarantee they'll be needed!) and improve what you've got because you are not perfect (again, sorry). It is better to find out what needs attention before you go to press rather than print 100 copies of something that will become nothing but a doorstop.

In this section, we'll look at ways to get feedback. While you may have wonderfully supportive friends and family who want you to succeed with your writing, what do they know about literature? Will they be honest or tell you what they think you want to hear? No one wants to hurt their best friend's feelings by telling them Chapter 2 didn't make sense or the manuscript was dull. So, when testing the waters, choose wisely.

Beta Readers

This is a person or people who read your manuscript before it is published. The age of a beta reader will vary. If you write a novel for middle-grade readers (aged 8 - 12 years), you might ask a small group of 8 – 12 year olds to read your novel and give their feedback. Or ask a teacher to read it.

Talking to your target audience could give insight you hadn't considered. You might ask them to complete a short questionnaire after reading: what they liked/disliked, is it the sort of book they could imagine other children reading, did you find it easy to understand/

follow, etc. If your beta readers are children or young adults, don't ask them technical questions; they won't know what you're talking about. Ask them for feelings.

Try to find readers interested in your genre and generally enjoy reading. Someone who doesn't read books (as opposed to graphic novels) regularly probably won't be able to give you too much constructive feedback—positive or negative. Similarly, if you ask a person to read your manuscript, give them guidelines. What do you want from them? Feelings, enjoyment, technical feedback? Be specific. And reiterate that you want them to be completely honest. Having a beta reader report that it's a good story and that they liked it isn't enough. What did they like? What makes it a good story? What didn't they like?

Talk to your library if you don't have people around you to ask and don't want to pay for beta readers. They may be able to put you in touch with local book clubs or writing groups. There are also plenty of other places to find beta readers online, such as Instagram influencers. Voracious Readers Only has an introductory offer where they will find 20 people to read and review your book for free. If you want further novels reviewed, it costs.

Manuscript Assessment

A knowledgeable person should write a manuscript assessment. If you have a friend who is an avid and informed reader, there's no reason why you couldn't ask them. You will need to set the parameters for them and can use the below as your starting point.

The alternative is paying a professional for an assessment. Again, the cost can be negotiated. They may not need to read the full MS to give you helpful feedback. Ask them to read the first XX pages (negotiate the number of pages with the assessor; I'd suggest 20 - 50). That may be enough to get feedback on the below categories.

Plot

Is there a beginning, middle and end, or is the plot cyclical? Are conflict and resolution present? Does the plot build or lag? Does the story have an interesting resolution/ending?

Story & Structure

Does the story flow well and pull the reader along with it? Does the text hold the reader's attention?

Text

Is the text correctly written and does it flow well? Or will the reader stumble over its construction? Is the text too wordy, slowing the pace and creating confusion? Does the text show, not tell?

Characters

Are the characters interesting and attractive to the reader? Are they well-fleshed out? Are the characters sympathetic/do they provoke a strong reaction?

Creativity & Originality

Is the work creative and inspiring? Is it clever, funny, fascinating? Is the work 'different' and original? Does it challenge the reader and advance the genre?

Suitability

Is the subject matter age-appropriate? Is it genre-appropriate?

Grammar & Punctuation

Does the author need to work on their grammar, punctuation and presentation, or is it spot-on?

Readiness

Is this manuscript ready to be submitted to a publisher?

Picture books

Does the subject matter hold illustration potential? Does the text allow the illustrations to do to the talking? Are the illustrations well done?

Notes/Recommendations

Most assessors will finish the assessment with notes covering the good or well-done aspects of the story and recommendations to consider. This could be anything from slight changes in setting or character to possible publishing or marketing options to consider.

Find a Community

Writing is a solitary experience. However, we're not meant to operate in isolation. Join a book club. Find the local writers' group. Interact with other writers and readers. This gives you a community to bounce ideas around with, share knowledge and information and further your writing skills and capabilities. Many local writing groups hold competitions. Submit a short story or poem for the experience. You never know, you may win.

Trying to do everything yourself or in isolation can be hard work. Meeting with like-minded people can be a great resource for gaining knowledge and making connections.

Get Reviews

This might be putting the cart before the horse, but let's go there.

You've asked your beta readers to give you feedback. You've had your MS assessed. You've probably asked Aunty Mary to read it, too. This is where family and friends can get involved. Have any of them made remarks you could use for marketing or pitching? If you are planning a pre-release advertising campaign, including reviews from reputable readers can carry some weight. For example, you've written a middle-grade reader, why not ask the local grade 6 teacher to read it and write a review? Or take a copy of your romance novel to the library and see if one of the staff would read and review it.

List your novel on Goodreads (once it's published, of course) and ask for reviews. Social media influencers may be an option. Reviews are recommendations that will increase your sales. So shop around friends, family, acquaintances, members of your book club or writers' group, local library staff, and ask for reviews. I've found people are generally lazy (myself included), so they may tell you they enjoyed your story but not put it in writing. If someone says, "Wow, I couldn't put the book down!" ask them if they'd write a short review or if you can quote them. Every little bit helps.

Reedsy offers a 'Discovery' service. Submit your book, and for $50, they will review it and, if they like it, add it to their 'Discover List.' You gain exposure and reviews.

Writer Goals

By identifying writing goals, wading your way through the reams of information on publishing will be easier as you know where you want to go and what options you can investigate further.

Writer Goals

Writing goals is like following a recipe. You want to bake. You know the ingredients you need. Now, you need to work out the process or order they must go in to end up with a cake.

At the end of the last chapter, the activity was writing your goals. Think about this again and consider the following.

As a writer:

• where do you want to go with your writing? Professional, semi-professional, hobby.

• what type of publishing do you see yourself doing?

• can you / do you want to learn about the publishing industry so you can make informed decisions?

• what are your strengths and weaknesses?

• how much time can you dedicate to polishing your writing?

• what obstacles stand in the way?

• in the perfect world, where do you see your writing career (professional or amateur) in five years?

Revisiting these questions, have you learned anything new about yourself and your aspirations? What would you like to change within your writing practice? What steps do you need to take to get where you want to go? It may be as simple as finding a local writing group to get involved with so you can bounce ideas around, find beta readers, or a community of like-minded people. Or maybe you need further study to become a better writer.

SMART Goals

Use the SMART acronym to make them clear.

- **S** Specific - It needs to be focused and specific. Try to avoid being too abstract or broad. Remember, you're honing in on where you're going.

- **M** Measurable - It's important to track your goals to know you're progressing. The specific goal you've set needs a measurable component. If it doesn't, you may need to rework the goal. Remember, you're being specific.

- **A** Achievable - there's no point in setting yourself the goal of having your novel published by Penguin Random House by the end of the year. It's specific. It's measurable. But it's not something you can control. Keep your goals within your control. Otherwise, you may be setting yourself up to fail, hindering your progress.

- **R** Relevant - ensure your goals move you forward.

- **T** Timely - set yourself a reasonable timeline to complete your goal.

ACTIVITY THREE: Goal Setting

How you choose whether to pitch to an agent, a publisher, or self publish will depend on your goals. What do you want to achieve as a writer? This builds on the first activity of knowing who you are. What do you want to achieve?

Think of yourself as a business. You need a plan.

- What do you want to achieve NOW? ______________________
  ____
  ____
  ____
- What do you want to achieve in the future? _______________
  ____
  ____
  ____
- What resources (time and money) do you have to invest in your business? ____
  ____
  ____
  ____
- How do you want to achieve it? __________________________
  ____
  ____
  ____

Remember, there are no right or wrong answers here. There is no limit to the reach of your goals. Be honest, dream big (or small) and visualise your future.

Things You Need To Know and Consider

A BRIEF HISTORY

Publishing for a mass audience has been around for centuries. Where, once upon a time, publications were for a select few, things began to change in 1040 when China invented the world's first type-printing technology. Since then, we've progressed in leaps and bounds.

- 1534 Cambridge University Press founded by Henry VIII (oldest known publisher)
- 1811 Jane Austen paid a publisher to print Sense and Sensibility
- 1979 Birth of desktop publishing
- 1997 Birth of Print on Demand (POD)
- 1999 digital era begins
- 2004-2007 E-Readers and self-publishing arrives
- Print on Demand
- No need to print 1000 copies and hope you sell them
- Scribus, Scribd, Smashwords
- Lulu
- Audiobooks

In the 21st century, there are a plethora of publishing options and selling platforms: traditional publishing houses, dependant publishers, vanity press, hybrid publishers, self-publishing, online sales, ebooks, physical books, audio books. My advice, keep it simple to start with. You can always expand on your formats in time. Ponder the type of publisher (traditional, hybrid or self) to begin with, as this will also affect whether ebooks or audio books need to be considered.

BOOK SUPPLY CHAIN

The steps and people that make up the book supply chain can be extensive. When thinking about publishing, it goes beyond whether to submit to a publishing house, self-publish or approach a hybrid publisher. You need to have given some thought to your writing goals. Do you want to be a full-time writer where this is your career? Do you want to publish a memoir for the family? Or maybe it's a poetry book for your local poetry group. Assuming you want global domination, let's look at the Book Supply Chain and the links between them. Their functions differ and may or may not be relevant depending on what you're publishing and why.

First, we have the **author** – without an author, there is not book! Arguably, this is changing, with some using artificial intelligence to write. However, it still comes back to someone inputting the information to create a story and (preferably) reading and editing what the AI spits out. So, our author writes the draft manuscript - a little obvious, I know. You probably wouldn't be here if you didn't have, or weren't working on, a manuscript you want to become a book.

A **Literary agent** – acts on behalf of an author to find a 'home' with a publisher. Many publishers state, "No unsolicited manuscripts will be accepted." That means they will only talk to agents.

An agent has extensive knowledge of and networks in the publishing industry. Generally, an author pitches their novel to an agent who decides whether they are taking on new clients, whether the manuscript is at a standard the industry expects, and which publisher(s) to approach and negotiate for the author. They do the leg work, the hustling and attract interest to 'sell' the author as much as the manuscript.

An **Editor** edits or fine-tunes a manuscript. Agents and publishers will want to see a good draft before considering taking you on.

Editors come in all shapes and sizes. Their roles vary depending on the type of editing to be undertaken. It may include proofreading, structural editing and story development, to name a few. Their job is to create the best version of the manuscript before it goes into production. While a traditional publisher will go over a manuscript with a fine-tooth comb, correcting grammatical errors and making suggestions to improve the story, having your manuscript edited before trying to get it published is invaluable. I'll cover this more in a later chapter.

Design – This incorporates a book's interior and exterior appearance: page format, book size, internal images, font, headers/ footers, front and back cover colours and illustration/image(s), spine, and blurb.

A graphic designer usually works on the cover design while the interior needs to be formatted to be genre/audience appropriate.

Production – formatting files (based on design brief). The production of the book takes the interior and exterior design and formats it for print or electronic release (ebook).

Printing – as the word suggests, it's the physical production of the book to be distributed.

Marketing – promotion of the book. A marketing department works on a strategy for promoting and selling the book. For example, how to get the most copies off the shelves and into people's hands. This could be ad campaigns, public speaking campaigns, or interviews on radio or television.

Distribution – circulating books to retail outlets, libraries or other distribution points (e.g. wholesalers). This may be an online or physical book store, library, national distribution, global distribution.

Retail –point-of-sale outlets. This is the store(s) where books will be sold.

Customers – the ones that will buy your book. The reader(s). I could spend a lot of time breaking down each of the steps involved in all of this – and some of the steps I will cover – but I want to give you the broad brushstrokes to better understand the processes and industry. The aim is to give you the basic information to make an informed decision on which publishing path best suits you and your manuscript. Or what further research you need/want to complete to make an informed decision.

Most of the list applies to all publishing types. However, the 'agent' only applies to traditional publishing. Each has a brief explanation or description to help you identify where you might need to outsource for help or learn skills you don't currently have.

What is a Publishing House?

As the term suggests, a publishing house is where your private work is converted from a word document on your computer or handwritten manuscript to become a public document available to the masses.

Traditionally (prior to the 19th century), this would see a writer take their manuscript to a printer and pay them to format and print copies for resale—basically, self-publishing. However, the industrial revolution of the 19th century brought the machination of the printing press and mass production. Publishing became more specialised allowing authors to concentrate on the writing and publishers to concentrate on the selling.

In the 21st century, there are an abundance of options for writers to pursue and all come with pros and cons: perception, stigma, costs, ease of access, audience, distribution channels, etc.

All publishing options are based on different funding source—i.e. who pays to have a manuscript published. A traditional publisher like Penguin Random House takes the funding risk. The author isn't out of pocket for expenses as the publisher pays for editing, formatting, cover designs, printing, distribution, market, etc. and shares any profit with the author.

All traditional publishers are based on the size of their market share —and, generally, the size of organisation. The Big 5 in book publishing control 80% of the market.

Examples of publishing houses are:
- The Big 5: Penguin Random House, MacMillan, Simon & Schuster, Harper Collins, Hachette
- Medium to Large – Hay House, Pegasus
- Small Press – Ford St, Pantera Press, Affirm Press

Cost Breakdown for Traditional Publishing

How much it costs to produce a book is a little like asking how long is a piece of string. It depends. However, there are some things we can calculate.

You often hear the amount returned to an author is a pittance compared to the recommended retail price of a book. That's because each link in the supply chain wants its cut. The breakdown of this is as follows:

• Agent	10% – 15%*
• Bookstore	25% – 40 %
• Distribution	20%
• Printer	10%
• Publishing House	10%
• Author	10%

*The agent's commission comes out of the Author's 10%.

So, for a $30 book sold through the local bookstore, you're looking at this break down of where that money goes.

• Bookstore – 25% – 40 %	$15.00
• Distribution – 20%	$ 6.00
• Printer – 10%	$ 3.00
• Publishing House – 10%	$ 3.00
• Author – 10%	$ 3.00
	$30.00

*The agent's commission of 0.45 cents per book will come from the author's $3.00. So, the Author actually only makes $2.55.

This gives an idea of the return on investment (ROI) with a traditional publisher. The return seems minimal when you think about the time and effort it has taken to write a manuscript—best selling or not.

What does this suggest?

In a crude nutshell, publishing is all about making money for the business stakeholders. It's not about pleasing the author. Not about just appealing to readers. It's not about the art or making the manuscript the best it can be. It is all about the stakeholders in the supply chain and their ROI.

Have you noticed how many already famous people are becoming authors? Professional athletes, TV personalities, film stars, Royalty!? It's because there's less risk for the publisher. They can almost guarantee that people will flock to buy the books.

When I published my first book, It's [Not] All About Liz!, I didn't have a large social media following or other claim to fame. I attended a workshop for wannabe authors run by Hay House, a huge publisher of people-focused narratives. They soon made it very clear that without an existing 'fan base' (if you like), I had almost no chance of being picked up by a publisher. It was too risky. They would have to put a lot of time, effort and money into promoting me in the hope that people warm to my subject matter and buy the book. It had nothing to do with the quality of the story written and everything to do with risk.

It sounds unfair, as the writer has put the most time and effort into creating the masterpiece that others will profit from, but keep in mind the publisher is taking all the financial risk and every step costs someone time and/or money.

As a new author attempting to enter the literary world and with many 'publishing' options open to authors these days, the question may be asked: Are publishers still relevant?

I would argue, absolutely! They take on the economic risk – I don't. There is the human capital they invest – trained professionals like graphic designers, printers, editors, etc. There is the Social Capital they invest – established relationships with distributors, retailers, etc. There is Intellectual Capital they invest – they know how to sell foreign rights or have books translated when most authors don't. They also have Symbolic

Capital – branding. This feeds into the stigma attached to self-publishing. If it's published through a traditional publisher, it's a "real" book.

Small Press

As the name suggests, a small press publisher has a smaller list of titles, thus a lower financial turnover, limited releases each year, and a smaller distribution network. They're more likely to cater to a niche market, such as a specific genre. Being small, they can be more flexibility and are (generally) more willing to take a risk if they think the story is good enough. The writer may get a small upfront payment (advance), but this is not guaranteed. They take on most of the financial risk—as other publishing houses—but their team may multitask between all production steps rather than dedicated to one task. Distribution may be limited and they may ask you to do more hands-on publicity.

If you're sitting there thinking, I don't have a large social media following, I'm not already famous, or I'm not even sure if my story is any good! Don't despair! All is not lost. It will mean a little more leg work and potentially learning new marketing skills, but it can be done and be successful. Still Alice by Lisa Genova was rejected by traditional publishers as the subject was a little dark and the reader audience small. It went on to be adapted for the screen. Legal Blonde by Amanda Brown was first published as print-on-demand before being sold to a publisher. And self-published writers can produce best-sellers. The Martian –Andy Weir – was turned by literary agents with previous novels. He decided to self-publish and sold 35,000 copies in the first three months – which then got the attention of publishers. Peter Rabbit – Beatrix Potter – rejected many times as publishers wanted Potter to make changes to her manuscript, which she didn't feel enhanced the story. Rich Dad Poor Dad – David Kiyosaki – decided to self-publish and sold 1,000 copies from the back of a friend's car. Three years later, the book made the New York Times best-seller list. E L James originally wrote 50 Shades of Grey as Twilight fanfiction. However, due to the explicit content it was reworked to become what it is today and was released as an ebook before becoming a print book.

Being rejected by publishers is something every writer needs to get comfortable with. The reasons publishers put manuscripts on the 'slush pile' varies and are not always because they are poorly written.

Look at this list.

- Gone With the Wind – Margaret Mitchell
- The Wonderful Wizard of Oz – L. Frank Brown
- Lord of the Flies – William Golding
- Moby Dick – Herman Melville
- Dune – Frank Herbert
- A Wrinkle in Time – Madeline L'Engle
- Carrie – Stephen King
- Harry Potter and the Philosopher's Stone – J K Rowling
- Kon-tiki – Thor Heyerdahl
- The Princess Diaries – Meg Cabot
- A Time To Kill – John Grisham
- Little Women – Louisa May Alcott

All rejected. Some iconic titles that authors didn't give up on even if publishers did.

Self-Publishing – What is it?

In the past, publishers were driven by quality writing. You would most likely get a publishing deal if you were a good writer. However, that's no longer the case. Good stories are being put in the slush pile all the time. So, what other options are available to writers?

In 2000, Stephen King – the first major author to self-publish a book online – declared, "My friends, we have the chance to become Big Publishing's worst nightmare." With advances in technology, the publishing industry has and continues to change.

Self-publishing means taking on all elements of publishing a manuscript:

- Editing
- Design
- Marketing

- Production
- Printing
- Distribution
- Retail
- Customer

If you self-publish, you'll need to learn how to:

- Write a query letter
- Format for publishing
- Produce additional information

Self-publishing requires the author to cover the full expense of printing, publishing, and distribution of the novel.

Hybrid/Vanity Press

Hybrid and/or Vanity Publishing sizes vary considerably. They may be a one-person option willing to take on any project for a fee.

Hybrid or Vanity Press is similar to self-publishing, but rather than needing to be a jack of all trades, so whether your book sells doesn't overly affect them. You pay for their services to produce your book and look after distribution. While going down the Hybrid/Vanity Press route gets your story off your computer and out into the world, I urge some caution. Fees are paid upfront (by you) and there may be little incentive for them to sell your book. They've made their money.

Hybrid/Vanity Press is almost a dirty word in the industry, as so many dodgy players are out there. Anyone with some computer nouse can set themselves up as a hybrid press. They tell a writer what they want to hear, promise the world but deliver very little. Horror stories abound! I know a writer who paid $18,000 to have his book published. That's a lot of books they will need to sell just for the writer to break even!

That might be harsh or overly critical of Hybrid publishers. Not because I think hybrid publishers don't have a valid part to play in publishing but because I know of too many rogue agencies offering services at exorbitant costs for minimal work. I want authors to do their research when it comes to hybrid publishers. There are some decent ones out there, but they are few and far between. And what most of them won't tell authors is that a lot of what they offer, the author could do themselves. They will provide editing, design, marketing, production, and distribution, but they come at a cost.

Vanity or hybrid press is similar to self-publishing in as much as the author pays for the production of the book. However, the publisher may assist with some aspects of the production, such as cover design, distribution, or editing.

A Dependent publisher has financial backers. Again, the author won't be out of pocket for expenses. However, the dependent publisher may acquire the work by paying a one-off fee to the author and keeping any profit in full. Or a contract will outline the profit split between the author and publisher. A dependent publisher may be genre-specific, such as fitness.

All are based on a Market Sector. This may be commercial trade, education (textbooks), academic and professional, or genre-specific (e.g., romance).

When looking at the various roles and responsibilities in the book chain supply, there are financial implications for the writer.

A word of warning before we move on. Whichever publishing route you take, if contracts are involved, ensure you read them thoroughly. Or, better still, ask someone who understands contracts to read them.

ISBNs, BISACs and Literary Agents

Your manuscript is done! It's edited, been read by beta readers, feedback taken onboard, and proofread. Now, it's time to get it out to the public.

In this chapter, we'll look at the publishing steps and things to consider.

Literary Agents

Literary agents are wonderful. They do all the legwork, taking your manuscript and shopping it around publishers. An agent is almost mandatory if you want to go down the traditional publishing route. So, where do you find one? Google, Australian Society of Authors, state writing bodies, and independent websites. One site with a free list of agents (and many other helpful writing tips) is Reedsy: https://blog.reedsy.com/literary-agents/au/. Their list links to agents' websites and information.

To approach an agent, you will need to write a Query Letter.

This should:

- be no longer than one page (3 paragraphs)
- address the agent by their first name
- 2 - 3 sentences pitch of your novel (similar to a hook)
- address why you think they are a good fit for you
- short bio (focus on your writing, not your life story - unless it's relevant)

It should not include:

- family reviews of your manuscript
- more than one novel
- how wonderful everyone thinks you are (no bragging or false bravado)
- a pitch for a genre the agent doesn't represent.

Do your homework and research the right agent(s) to approach.

ISBNs

An ISBN is an International Standard Book Number. It is a unique identifier for commercially sold books. If you produce different formats such as hardcover, paperback, ebook, and audiobook, each will need a unique identifier. Having a unique identifier means retailers, libraries, or people can search your book with precision.

When self-publishing, many sites will offer a free ISBN for your book. However, beware. Many companies offering self-publishing services do not have 'searchable' ISBNs. That means if a bookstore within Australia searches for your novel produced overseas using the ISBN, they may not locate it. They can't sell it in their store if they can't find it.

While we all like something for free, spending a few dollars to buy a legitimate, searchable ISBN could be better. In Australia, that is through Thorpe-Bowker. One ISBN costs $44 (April 2023), or you can purchase ten for $88. Once you purchase it, you can pay an extra fee to download a barcode with the ISBN. However, search the internet for a 'barcode generator' and you can probably get a free barcode to add to your cover. Buy the ISBN! But not necessarily the barcode (personal choice). These ISBNs will be searchable globally.

BISAC Codes

A BISAC code is another form of identification for your novel. In a similar way to the ISBN identifying your specific book, the BISAC - a 9-

character alphanumeric code - identifies the category and subcategories of your book. Classifying your novel as fiction is general. It's more specific to classify it as historical fiction and even more precise to classify it as fiction/historical/fantasy. This information is important for booksellers and libraries when deciding whether to stock or list your novel or not.

So why do you, the author, need to know this? Several reasons. On many self-publishing websites, they will ask you to choose several BISAC codes (so they know where to list it on their website). Going into the local bookstore to see if they'll stock your book, you will probably be asked whatever category your book falls into. Remember, if you aspire to be a professional writer, you need to look professional. Creating marketing material such as an Additional Information sheet or even writing a query letter to an agent or publisher, if you know the BISAC code for your novel, you're saving someone time working it out, they'll be impressed and be more open to talking with you. We'll cover the additional information sheet and query letter in another section. For now, back to BISAC codes.

BISAC codes become a bit of rabbit warren - go down one hole to find the heading code—e.g. Fiction, then another for a subheading or subcategory, then another for a sub-subcategory. But it doesn't need to be too extensive. Usually, a heading code and two subheading codes are sufficient.

There are region-specific codes, but you don't need to go into that much detail for most novels. You can learn more about the codes from BISG - Book Industry Study Group. They provide a full list of the Headings, Subheadings, codes and explanations.

As a publishing consultant, some of the first questions I ask a prospective client are:

1/ Who is your audience?

2/ What is your book's genre?

3/ What age are your readers?

How someone answers these questions tells me all I need to know about how informed they are as writers. It can also indicate whether a traditional publisher will put them straight on the slush pile or take the time to read on. Know your stuff!

Formatting

Most manuscripts are written using some form of word processor. Even if the draft is written with pen and paper, it will need to be transposed into a document at some point. Formatting will depend on what you are doing with the manuscript. Are you approaching a publishing house? Or are you preparing it for self-publication?

In this section, we'll look at formatting for a publishing house, formatting for self-publication and software available to do the formatting.

Formatting for a Publishing House

If you are submitting to a publishing house, you won't need to do any special formatting. Most publishers list their guidelines stating how they want it presented: double-spacing, 12-point font, Garamond font, etc. They will also stipulate whether they want it as a PDF or a Word document. Check publishers' websites and make sure you follow their style guide. Even selling a short story or feature article to a magazine will require a format.

Grammarly

While not exactly formatting software, Grammarly is a great way to have your MS checked for grammar and spelling. You tell Grammarly what the domain of the document is - academic, business, general, creative writing, etc. - your writing intention - inform, storytelling, etc - who your audience is - general, knowledgeable, expert - and formality. Grammarly then checks the document using these guidelines.

There is a free version available that allows you to upload your document and check basic correctness, clarity, engagement and tone. Or you can subscribe for a more thorough assessment with recommendations.

Formatting For Self-Publishing

If you want to self-publish, there is software for formatting. The following programs allow for physical book and ebook publications.

InDesign

Adobe InDesign is the industry standard publishing software that allows you to format a range of publications. It comes with many standard layouts and templates. Or you can start from scratch with a blank page and set all the parameters you want. There's not much you can't design with it! The program has many features that will allow you to be as finicky as you wish. This is great if you have graphics to include, but may be more than you need for a text document.

Being such a comprehensive app, it may take some time to learn and understand. However, the help function within the software is extensive and includes video clips to help you learn.

You can sign up for a free trial of InDesign or take out an ongoing subscription costing $29.99 per month (April 2023).

If you plan on creating many publications or want the best of the best, InDesign is the way to go. Just allow yourself plenty of time to learn it. It has a lot of bells and whistles.

Scribus

Scribus is a great option if you're not ready to jump in the deep end and play with the big kids on InDesign. It's a free forever open-source program that comes with templates, will let you format text, add images, and everything else you need to create the interior of your novel. Scribus has many templates, including US Trade size 6" x 9" template, or you can create from scratch to fit any page size. All you need to do is add your text and/or images.

Unfortunately, the help function in Scribus isn't as good as InDesign, but you can find tutorials on YouTube.

On a personal note, I have both InDesign and Scribus. It may be because I learnt Scribus while at university, but I find navigating it a lot easier. It isn't as fancy as InDesign or has the same variety of templates, but it's all I need as most of my manuscripts text based for US Trade. Like any software, it will drive you crazy at times and may be clunky, but it works just fine.

Other Options

Depending on the platform you choose to create your book (covered in another section), many come with tools for publishing. The major ebook sites are KDP Amazon, Barnes & Noble, Ingram Sparks and Lulu. Some allow you simply to upload a PDF and they do the rest. Others, like Lulu, require you to upload a formatted PDF.

There are other options available if you want to do some internet searching. Each will be slightly different and have pros and cons. Most of the final decision will come down to what you're publishing, how often you'll publish and what program you find user-friendly.

I haven't spoken about audiobooks, as this requires a lot more consideration. You need to decide who will read, record and produce your novel. You can do it yourself if you have the basic recording and production equipment and a soundproof booth (which can be a cupboard), but it's beyond the scope of this book.

Self-Publishing Sites

Self-publishing is taking off in a similar manner to the indie music industry. Artists are tired of playing by the rules of large production companies that dictate the terms. Technology advances make it easier for artists to keep control and produce what they want in the manner they want.

In this section, we'll look at several of the top self-publishing sites. It is not an extensive look, but more a tip-of-the-iceberg look to compare pricing, royalties, and reach.

Amazon KDP (Kindle Direct Publishing)

Amazon KDP is arguably the leader in self-publishing. Originally publishing only eBooks, they've also branched out into physical books. And, being part of the Amazon juggernaut, your book will appear in their bookstore.

Once an account is set up, you follow a list of prompts to choose your format, input your information, and upload your manuscript. They have a cover creator, or you can upload a file you created elsewhere. It is relatively user-friendly, but if you get stuck, they have great support (real people!).

Pricing: it's free to upload and create your book.

Royalties: 70% on eBooks priced between $2.99 and $9.99, or 35% for eBooks priced below $2.99. 60% on paperbacks.

Production costs: A book with 24 - 108 pages costs $4.49 to print. Books with 110 - 828 pages cost $2.17 + 0.0215 cents per page.

Barnes & Noble

Barnes & Noble Press has a similar publishing process. Pick your format and follow the step-by-step guides to prepare and upload your files. However, cover creation with B&N isn't as easy as other sites.

On the plus side, B&N is a major distributor worldwide. Though they have lost some traction in recent years with the rise of Amazon, they are still one place where you want your book listed for sale.

Pricing: it's free to upload and create your book.

Royalties: 70% on eBooks priced over $0.99. 55% less printing/ production costs on physical books.

Production costs: These depend on book size, paper quality, colour or B&W, etc. However, their calculator lets you play with scenarios. I entered the following data: B&W interior on a cream page, paperback 201 - 250 pages, which I sell for $10.00. The printing cost was $4.22. Therefore, the Royalty of 55% = $5.50 less print costs of 4.22, leaving me with $1.28 in my pocket. Regardless of book size, they withhold 45% for 'Retail & Distribution'.

IngramSparks

IngramSparks is another popular option for publication. This is mainly because of their distribution channels. As with other sites, they use a step-by-step process to prepare your book.

Pricing: $49.00 per title for eBooks and physical books.

Royalties: This is difficult to calculate as they call it 'Publisher Compensation'. They have a calculator, which may help.

Everything with IngramSparks seems like asking, 'How long is a piece of string?' It depends. Rather than try to explain it, I suggest visiting their website to see if it will work for you.

Lulu.com

Lulu is an online publisher that flies under the radar in Australia and yet is a great starting point for printing physical books. They have a variety of publication types to choose from (novels, comics, magazines, photobooks, eBooks, etc.), as well as varying sizes within the different categories.

Pricing: free to upload.

Royalties: 90% on eBooks. 80% less production costs on physical books.

Production costs: as with other sites, this will depend on book size and format. However, you can play with the pricing calculator on the home page. Word of Warning! If you want to play with pricing, I strongly recommend you create an account to get accurate postage and tax costs in your currency. If you aren't logged into an account, you will still get a ballpark figure, usually in USD, but it will be more accurate if they know where you are in the world. And always treat the pricing as a ballpark. It may change slightly when you actually produce a book.

On Lulu's landing page are options to play with: products, writer resources and an online bookstore. It's much easier to find out the important stuff, like costs, right on their landing page.

There are templates with page formatting information. So, when you're in Scribus, InDesign or other software, you know exactly what information to enter to get the size and format you need to publish with Lulu.

Another resource I like about Lulu is the ability to create a basic cover (not too fancy) with the cover creation tool or upload a cover you have designed elsewhere. I like using Canva.com (a graphic design website) to create book covers, as endless options exist. If you've never used Canva, check it out. You can design everything from book covers to social media posts, book trailers to logos.

The issue with all online self-publishing sites is the postage costs. However, you can play with the pricing function to get an idea of printing and/or postage costs before you create a book.

One thing a hybrid publisher will try to sell you is 'global distribution'. Global distribution means your book will be listed on Amazon, Gardiners, and Barnes & Noble - some of the biggest book distributors worldwide. With Lulu and most other self-publishers, global distribution is something you choose with the click of a button. It is not something hybrid publishers have exclusive access to.

Other Platforms

I'm listing basic information about other platforms for you to research, as I am less familiar with them. These platforms range from physical books, eBooks, audiobooks and aggregators.

Apple Books - Pricing: Free to upload. Royalties: 70% on most books.

Rakuten Kobo - Pricing: Free to upload. Royalties: 70% on eBooks priced over $2.99 in the US or 45% for books priced below $2.99.

Draft2Digital - Pricing: 10% of the book's retail price.

Smashwords - 15% of retail price is on the Smashwords platform, and 10% is on other platforms.

ACTIVITY FOUR -Exploring The Sites

It's one thing for someone to pass on useful information; however, it can quickly become information overload. For this exercise, go to some of the publishing sites and have a play.

1/ What do you like/dislike? ______________________________

____

____

2/ Why? ____

____

____

3/ Would any of them help you reach your writer goals? _______

____

____

____

4/ How? ____

____

____

5/ What further research would you need to do? ____________

____

____

6/ How can you find answers to your research questions? ______

____

____

What Happens Next?

One of the keys to success in any industry is the ability to look professional. I like to say, "It's all about the bluff!" If you're starting out in your writing career and have worked through each section of the Writer's Resources, you may not feel like a professional yet. That's okay. It's time to learn a few more tricks that will help you look professional.

In this section, we'll look at support documents. Whether approaching a publisher or doing everything yourself, you will need to create an array of documents as part of your pitch. From query letters to press releases, author bios to story synopsis. Each serves a different purpose while overlapping with information.

As I go through the different sections, you'll see a lot of crossover. If you hear a term and aren't quite sure what it is, don't worry too much; it will probably be covered elsewhere.

Author Bio

The author bio is often the most challenging thing for a writer to create. How do you summarise yourself in 3 or 4 short sentences or paragraphs? It's a challenge! How much personal information should you include? I'd err on the side of not much. If this goes with a pitch or submission, it should be short and show your writing abilities. Keep it short.

Include: your writing history, publishing history, what you do outside of writing (hobbies, work, immediate family).

Don't include: contact details (they're listed elsewhere) or full life history, i.e. schools, moves around the country, family pet, etc.

You may need several versions of the author bio. If you're submitting to a publisher, they may require a bio of 50 words, while pitching to a magazine may require something a little more substantial. Write the basics. You can always pad it out if needed for a different arena.

Synopsis or Overview

(See page 62 for example)

The synopsis is another document that might need several versions. If pitching to a publisher, check the submission guidelines on length. Some may want a 100-word synopsis; others may want 1000 words. If there is no word limit, keep it to no more than one side of an A4 page.

Include:

1. What the story is about in a nutshell (plot points but told in sentences, not bullet points).
2. The 1st paragraph should always include a hook - The story is about character who event/action because he or she wants something tangible but complication.
3. Broad brush strokes of where the story goes.

The overview is a more in-depth synopsis. It covers the above and includes additional information.

1. Audience and why someone would want to read the book
2. Why/how this book is different to others in the market
3. Key selling points
4. Marketing highlights
5. Author Bio

Query Letter

Whether you pitch to a publisher or a retail outlet, a query letter must address specific points, be succinct and not waffle. You may only have a small window of opportunity, so give as much information as possible.

Here is a structure to use as your guide.

1. Who are you sending your letter to? Be specific. Address a person by name if you know it or use the term 'Editor'. Not generic (Dear Sir/Madam or To whom it may concern).

2. 1st paragraph - include the hook. Your hook should be 2-3 sentences summarising your story to entice readers to want to know more. Here is a good way to think about your hook. The story of a character who event/action because he or she wants something tangible but complicated. e.g. Eleven-year-old Shayla will have to join forces with an Aboriginal wizard (she doesn't know exists), use powers (she doesn't know she has), and enter a world (she doesn't think is real) in order to rescue her fifteen-year-old sister, Willow. *(The Land of Giant Pineapples*).

3. Next paragraph(s) - What is your story about? This is a summary overview of the plot points. It may be 2 or 3 paragraphs in length and gives the main points, not all the details.

It's okay to give away the ending.

4. What is your story really about? While the story may be an adventure, a love story, or a military saga, the real story may be the relationship between characters, finding a sense of self, or overcoming something that's held them back for years.

5. Previous publishing history. You may not have a publishing history if this is your debut novel. That's okay. Say, 'This is my debut novel'. Don't say what you think they want to hear. Be honest. Talk (briefly) about writing experiences.

6. Who is the author? Not your life story! You want one paragraph that introduces you, the author. Try to include things that may be relevant to your novel. For example, you've written a book of poetry based around a region. What's your connection with that region? Include where you're from, your qualifications, your interest in the subject matter, and where you live. Those sorts of things. No one has time to read about your childhood, what you do for work (other than a job title), or how you won the pub trivia contest 3 weeks in a row.

7. Comp Titles. A comp title is a comparison book. They're books that would have a similar audience or similar themes/genre. For example, the novel The Hunger Games would be a comp title for Maze Runner.

Try to keep your query letter to one side of an A4 page. If you write a draft that is two and a half pages long, it needs to be reduced. The purpose of the query letter is to gather interest Broad brush strokes covering who you are and what your book is about. If they want more information (and we hope they do), they'll ask for it.

Additional Information Sheet

(See Appendix B p 61 for example)

An Additional Information Sheet is a great way to show off your professionalism! It includes all the information a retailer/library/ promoter needs. Creating an Additional Information Sheet also means it's one less job for them to do.

The Additional Information has a set structure and information that needs to be included. Your page should have two panels. The right side panel will be approximately four centimetres in width and the left side panel approximately thirteen centimetres in width (plus page margins).

Left Panel information

1. Book Title - Bold, size 16 font for both the heading and the title

2. Author(s) - Bold, size 14 font for heading and regular, size 12 font for name(s).

3. Illustrator - Bold, size 14 font for heading and regular, size 12 font for name(s).

4. Hook - Bold, size 14 font for heading and regular, size 12 font for hook.

5. Blurb - Bold, size 14 font for heading and regular, size 12 font for blurb.

6. Key Selling Points - Bold, size 14 font for heacing. Use dot pots (regular, size 12 font) to list selling points. E.g. characters are indigenous and non-indigenous, themes are contemporary, and themes vary from environmental issues to reconciliation; teachers' notes are available for class lessons on themes.

7. Audience - Bold, size 14 font for heading. Use dot points (regular, size 12 font) to list the audience. E.g. readers aged 8 - 12 years who enjoy fantasy and magic, educators with an interest in environmental issues, readers of Harry Potter.

8. Author Bio(s) - Bold, size 14 font for heading and regular, size 12 font for bio

9. Comp Titles - Bold, size 14 font for heading. List three comp titles in regular, size 12 font. The information for each comp title should include book title (italic font), year of publication, author, format, number of pages, ISBN, Publisher and (if possible) top Amazon ranking. Here's an example.

Percy Jackson and the Olympians: the lightning thief, (2005), Rick Riordan, paperback, 384 pages, ISBN # 9780141329994, Penguin Books Ltd. Top Amazon ranking #6

10. Marketing Highlights - Bold, size 14 font for heading. Use dot points (regular, size 12 font) to list Marketing Highlights. E.g. Large poster advertising on the back of school buses; purchase in-store promotional stands with Dymocks; school appearances during Book Week in primary schools; book trailer appearing on social media.

11. Publishing House History - Bold, size 14 font for heading and regular, size 12 font for information. If you're traditionally published or self-published, include their information here. E.g. Allen&Unwin is Australia's leading independent publisher and has been voted "Publisher of the Year" thirteen times... (You can find this information on the publisher's website). If self-published, refer to what site you used and general information about the process.

Right Panel information

1. Image of the book cover - this is a thumbnail image of the book cover

2. Publishing date - Bold, size 9 font for heading and regular, size 9 font for date. E.g. Sempter, 2021

3. Price - Bold, size 9 font for heading and regular, size 9 font for Price(s). If you have different formats, include the different prices. E.g. Paperback $30.00, ebook $6.99

4. ISBN - Bold, size 9 font for heading and regular, size 9 font for ISBN. If you have different formats, include the ISBNs for each format.

5. Time size - Bold, size 9 font for heading and regular, size 9 font for size. The trim size is the size of the book. E.g. 6" x 9" or 10.5" x 10.5"

6. Format - Bold, size 9 font for heading and regular, size 9 font for format. E.g. Paperback, Hardcover, ebook, spiral bound

7. Pages - Bold, size 9 font for heading and regular, size 9 font for numbers e.g. 220

8. # and type of illustrations - Bold, size 9 font for heading and regular, size 9 font for information. E.g. Forty simple black and white 'freehand digital' sketches to start each chapter.

9. BISAC codes - Bold, size 9 font for heading and regular, size 9 font for information. E.g. JUV03700 Juvenile/Fantasy and Magic.

The Additional Information may be several pages long, but remember, this is a summary document, so try to be succinct with information and limit it to approximately two pages.

Press Release

(see page 63 for example)

There is no reason why you shouldn't be contacting newspapers, radio stations, or even television stations announcing your book's launch. However, reach out to the local media first. You have a better chance of being covered in smaller media than national media. And, if you're a debut novelist, being interviewed on community radio is a great way to become familiar with interviews. Then, when Channel 9 calls asking you to be on the Today Show, you will have had some practice.

A Press Release should be no more than one side of an A4 page, including a picture of the cover and 'who', 'what', 'where', and 'when' type information. Who is the author? What have they written? When is/was it published? This is a good chance to rehash the information you've already created: author bio, hook, brief synopsis (don't give everything away in a press release), where it's available, etc.

While you are promoting a book, a press release is also promoting the author. So feel free to spend a little more time talking about the author and their connection to a region (if you are going to the local newspaper) or the significance of this book and this author.

Format for a Press Release:

1. At the top of the page in capitals, 'PRESS RELEASE"

2. Image of the cover on the left and book information in line with the image. Include the basic information: Title, author, illustrator (if applicable), ISBN, Genre, Price, Publisher

3. About the Book

4. About the Author(s)

5. Contact details - how they can contact you for more information or an interview.

Marketing

Marketing is the umbrella that incorporates Advertising and Publicity. Advertising is paying for attention. And Publicity is given for free.

The four Ps of Marketing:

• Product - what you are selling

• Price - cost

• Place - where it can be purchased

• Promotion - marketing and advertising

Two types of marketing

• Push marketing - taking your product to the consumer e.g. retail outlets

• Pull marketing - getting the customer to seek out your product, eg advertising on television.

If you're new to marketing, you may lack confidence. But don't despair; you don't need to go and reinvent the wheel. Look at what others are doing and replicate it. Think, "Same, Same but Different". Think about what motivates you to purchase something.

The other thing to keep in mind is your audience. BE SPECIFIC! Saying your book is for an adult audience isn't enough. What age, socio-economic group, gender, marital status, family size, education, occupation, race... There are many variables you can use to identify your audience, and the more specific they are, the better. Yes, an adult of any age may read your book. However, you might find most of them are 35 - 50-year-old women who live in a particular region, drink red wine, and are about to be empty-nesters. That's specific. When you identify them like this, you can better tailor your marketing and promotional material to them.

Places to promote your book and self.

Personal website, book website, social media, radio stations, newspapers, personal blog, other people's blogs, ask for reviews.

Get involved with others.

Give book reviews, join local writers' groups, post snippets from your book on social media or offer them for free, start a mailing list, start a newsletter, submit to a newsletter, give away free copies, speak to local bookstores and libraries, create a contest, participate in trade shows, create a poster, study SEO (search engine optimisation).

These are ideas. You don't have to do them all, but give some a go. Promotion doesn't have to cost a lot of money. Yes, you can buy advertising space on social media, but you don't have to. Ask your friends to share posts about your book—cross-promote with other writers. The options are endless.

Book Launch

I strongly recommend that every author who releases a book holds a book launch. It can be as big or as intimate as you like. The thing a book launch should be is a celebration. You've done what so many people would like to do but haven't managed - you've written and published a book. (I'd love a dollar for every person who's said to me, "I reckon I could write a book, but...") By now, you know it's not easy. It takes a lot of hard work, commitment and time to produce something good. So why not celebrate?

A book launch can tick several boxes.

1. Promoting your book launch could pull in a few more sales
2. It raises your profile
3. If you're celebrating the launch personally, that energy will rub off on others, creating positive momentum (others will start talking about it)
4. You can invite the local paper along
5. You can turn it into a fundraiser for your charity

This is your time to play after all your hard work. Pat yourself on the back and enjoy your moment in the spotlight.

Sales Outlets

If you're traditionally published, you don't need to worry about this so much. But you may still like to try some of these options as well. Just check with your publisher first.

If you're self-published, take your book and Additional Information to the local bookshops, post office, retail outlets that sell books and have a chat with the manager. Many are happy to promote or sell local authors' book on commission. You will find some that look down their nose at you, but generally, you'll get a positive reception.

List your book for Global Distribution. Then distributors like Amazon, Barnes & Noble, Gardiners, etc will add it to their lists worldwide.

Get in touch with me at Jaymah. I'm happy to add your novel(s) to Jaymah's online bookstore (it's free, and all profits go back to you). I'm also more than happy to promote it on Jaymah's social media.

Bottom line with sales outlets, get out there and talk to retailers. There's no point having a box of books sitting in your spare room.

Libraries

Many local libraries are more than happy to list novels by local authors. Give them a call and ask for the Acquisitions Department. Find out when their financial year starts/ends, as many have a budget for purchasing books, so you want to know the best time to pitch to them.

Alternatively, if you want to try distributing them further afield, find a library distributor. They won't automatically list your book. They will want to see a physical copy of it and have a read or read through your synopsis, additional information, etc. If they like it, they'll list it and promote it with all the libraries they have relationships with.

Legal Deposit to National Archives

Under the Copyright Act (1968), one copy of everything published in Australia must be given to the National Library under the 'legal deposit provisions'. This includes self and hybrid publishing.

You are also required to deposit a copy with your local state or territory library. While it's a legal requirement, I think it's fantastic to think my work won't die when I do. Your work is adding to the nation's story.

For more details on Legal Deposits, visit the National Libraries of Australia website or find your state contact.

Making the Decision: Traditional, Hybrid or Self-Publishing

Deciding the best option for publishing is based on several considerations: the purpose of your project, writer goals, understanding of the publishing process, access to tools and resources, and ability/ desire to take the steps needed.

In this section, we'll recap the main differences between the publishing types and look at a few scenarios to help you decide. Remember, there is no right or wrong option. It's what you're comfortable with and feels right for you and your project.

Types of Publishing

A different way to look at 'Types of Publishing' is to consider the funding source.

• Traditional - these are the publishing houses that accept your manuscript and not only take responsibility for each step in the publishing process but also the financial risk.

• Dependent - these are more of a genre or themed publisher, such as Cancer Council. Often, the work is commissioned and has financial backing.

• Hybrid - is a publisher for hirer. The author pays a fee for their expertise and experience to bring a book to market.

• Self - the author goes through all publishing steps themselves (however, this may include outsourcing some steps, such as editing or cover design) to bring a book to market. They are fully responsible for the costs involved.

Implications

Publishing Houses are not trying to please the author alone.

It is ALL about ROI and stakeholders in the supply chain.

They are invested in the book's success for the financial reward.

Art and creativity have a minor place to play in decision-making.

Hybrid Publishers are not trying to please the author or appeal to the readers.

They receive payment for their service upfront (they've had their ROI).

What happens next is not their concern.

Art and creativity have a minor place to play in decision-making.

Self-publishers are the authors.

They want their book to be a success.

They won't get an ROI unless their book is a success.

Art and creativity are a large part of their decision-making.

Relevance of Traditional Publishers

After being introduced to the different publishing options, reviewing cost breakdowns between traditional and self publishing and seeing how you could do it yourself, it would be a fair question to ask: Are publishing houses still relevant?

Keep in mind publishing houses offer economic capital (money to invest in a writer or novel), Human capital (specialist staff for each step of the production process), Social capital (established relationships with distributors, retailers, etc.) and Intellectual capital (they know how to sell foreign rights or translate a book to other languages). And they have something very powerful - symbolic capital (branding).

Making a Choice

We've looked at types of publishing.

We've looked at the steps to publication.

We've looked at cost breakdowns and financial returns for authors (and publishers).

We've looked at resources for doing it yourself and where to get them.

The only other consideration is time. Is your project time-sensitive?

If so, a traditional publisher may not be the best option. They usually have their publications locked in months, if not years, in advance.

Revisit your writer goals.

• Where do you want to go?

• What are your timelines?

• What resources do you have to invest? 'Resources' isn't just money. It may be something you can swap with another person: skill, time, resource sharing, etc.

• What are realistic limitations that you need help with?

• Write your own list of Pros and Cons for each topic covered in this book.

There is a lot that goes into publishing a book. However, if you think about it systematically, write your action plan and keep an open mind, you can do it! As they say, information is power. You now have the basic information to get your started. Now, get out there and share your stories.

Appendix A – Writer Resources

Formatting for Print

Tutorial on YouTube with top 5 Graphic Design Programs (Open Source / Free) https://www.youtube.com/watch?v=t0yZJ-smyqQ

Formatting for print software - Scribus - https://www.scribus.net/downloads/

Scributs Tutorials – Lesson 1 Getting Started and User Interface

https://youtu.be/hMlT9C6xcDw?si=PvupftsC1nqSoID3

Graphic design app - Canva - https://www.canva.com/free/

ISBNs and BISAC Codes

ISBN – Thorpe-Bowker Identifier Services https://www.myidentifiers.com.au/

Barcode Generator https://barcode.tec-it.com/en

BISAC - https://www.bisg.org/complete-bisac-subject-headings-list

Understanding Bisac' - https://blog.lulu.com/bisac-what-it-is-and-why-it-matters/

BISG – Book Industry Study Group - https://www.bisg.org/complete-bisac-subject-headings-list

Author Resources to explore

Julian Wood Bookseller – library distribution Australia-wide

https://julianwoodbookseller.com.au/

Writer Associations – Geelong Writers, Writers Victoria, Australian Society of Authors

Competitions – they're everywhere! Google 'writing competitions'

Festivals – Melbourne - https://literarylistings.com/melbourne-literary-festivals-2023/

Regional Festivals- https://literarylistings.com/regional-victorian-literary-festivals-2022a/

SourceBottle - https://www.sourcebottle.com/

Freelance Writing - https://www.freelancewriting.com/

Self-Publishing Formula - https://learn.selfpublishingformula.com/

ACX – audiobook creation - https://www.acx.com/

Jaymah - https://www.jaymahpress.com.au/

Voracious Readers - https://voraciousreadersonly.com/

Goodreads - https://www.goodreads.com/about/us

Reedsy - https://reedsy.com/discovery/submit

National Library Legal Depository - https://www.nla.gov.au/using-library/services-publishers/legal-deposit

State Legal Depository - https://ned.gov.au/ned/contact

Appendix B – Example of documents

Widow, Runt and Orphan.

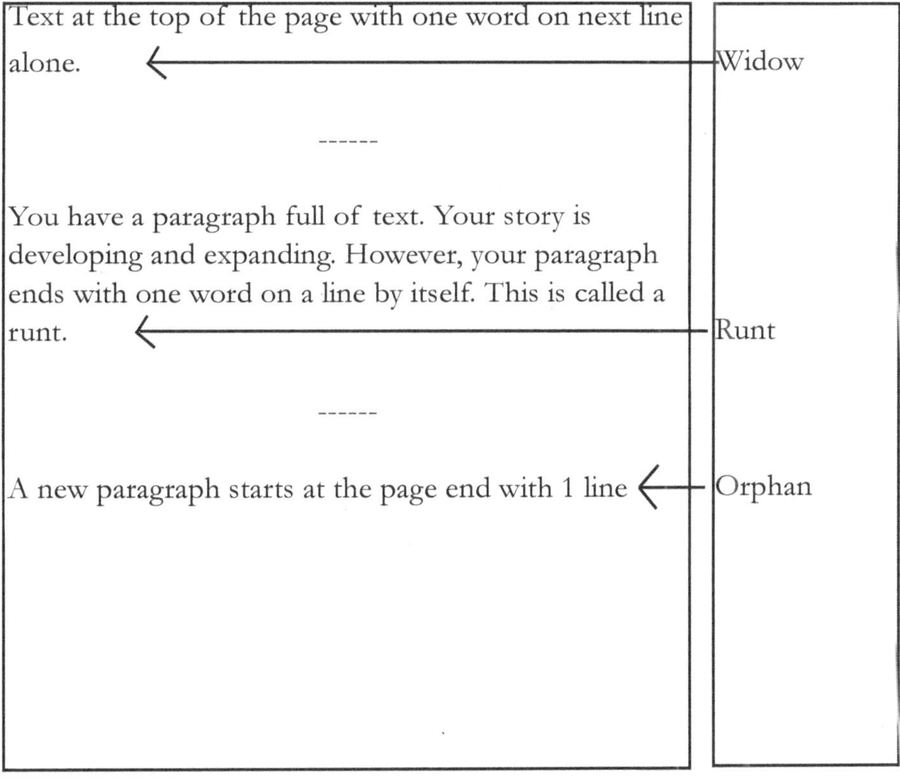

RIVER

A river occurs when text is justified with all lines being equal lengths. The space between words differs to make the lines equal in length, thus creating a 'visual' river. (The below has been exaggerated to give you the idea.)

Lorem ipsum Lorem ipsum Lorem ipsum Lorem ipsum Lorem ipsum lorem ipsum lorem ipsum lorem ipsum lorem ipsum lorem ipsum Lorem ipsum Lorem ipsum Lorem ipsum Lorem ipsum Lorem ipsum Lorem ipsum Lorem ipsum lorum ipsum lorum ipsum Lorem ipsum Lorem ipsum Lorem ipsum Lorem ipsum Lorem ipsum lorem ipsum lorem ipsum lorem ipsum lorem ipsum lorem ipsum Lorem ipsum Lorem ipsum Lorem ipsum Lorem ipsum Lorem ipsum Lorem ipsum Lorem ipsum lorum ipsum lorum ipsum

Lorem ipsum Lorem ipsum Lorem ipsum Lorem ipsum Lorem ipsum lorem ipsum lorem ipsum lorem ipsum lorem ipsum lorem ipsum Lorem ipsum Lorem ipsum Lorem ipsum Lorem ipsum Lorem ipsum Lorem ipsum Lorem ipsum lorum ipsum lorum ipsum Lorem ipsum Lorem ipsum Lorem ipsum Lorem ipsum Lorem ipsum lorem ipsum lorem ipsum lorem ipsum lorem ipsum lorem ipsum Lorem ipsum Lorem ipsum Lorem ipsum Lorem ipsum Lorem ipsum Lorem ipsum Lorem ipsum lorum ipsum lorum ipsum

Additional Information Sheet

Book title:

Author name

HOOK

This is your 'elevator speech': 1–3 sentences describing what the book is, who it's for, and/or why the target audience will want to buy it.

BLURB

Approximately 4–6 sentences describing the book's concept, giving a summary of the content or plot, describing the goal of the book, detailing why it's unique and appealing, and/or stating how it addresses a problem or interest of the target audience.

TABLE OF CONTENTS

If applicable

KEY SELLING POINTS

- Emphasise unique characteristics of this book that differentiate it from the competition. Useful data points (e.g., market size, market growth) can be mentioned here. Be sure to mention who is writing the foreword/afterword here and include mention of any major endorsements.

AUDIENCE

- Describe the readers who are likely to buy this book. List at least 3 distinct audiences. Be as specific as possible. 'Everyone' and 'the general reader' are not helpful.

AUTHOR BIO

Include the author's credentials for writing the book (e.g., education, work history, interests, life experience) and previously published works. Include writing experience in all formats. Be sure to mention the author's career or life highlights, widely read blogs or columns, TV/radio shows, or other publishing successes. Also, list the city (or cities) where the author lives.

COMP TITLES

- Include full title, ISBN, format, pub date and any indication of sales/reception.
- Comp titles should be on a similar subject, have a similar editorial approach, share a BISAC code, and/or be shelved in the same book shop section as this book.

MARKETING HIGHLIGHTS

- These are the highlights of your marketing plan for the book.
- Include the dates of any events you mention.

PUBLISHING HOUSE HISTORY

What should booksellers know about this book's publishing house? What will inspire confidence or suggest the particular focus of your books?

Pub date: Month 20XX

Price:

ISBN-13:

Trim: W x H

Format:

Pages:

 # and type of illustrations: (n/a if none)

Special features: (delete if none)

BISAC codes:

AI Updated [illegible]

Page 1 of 1

Synopsis

Catalunya Trilogy: Book 1 - Catelina

Set in Barcelona, Catalunya, Spain, 1635 – 1659, we follow the events that begin the disin-tegration of the once independent Catalan state. Through the lives of the Mares and Amador families, the story tells of a David and Goliath type battle for continued independence.

There are five point of view characters: Catelina Mares (Catalunya personified); Ignasio (Nacho) Alonso (Spain personified); Louis Bouchard (France personified); Mateo Amador (love interest/Catalan independence personified); and Pau Mares (father/traditional Catalan personi-fied).

Beginning in 1635, naïve, fifteen-year-old Catelina first realises the Catalan way of life is under threat and must discover how to ward off those that threaten her and her nation.

Pau Mares, a successful merchant trader, sees staying with Catalunya's traditional ally (Spain) as the way forward. For the sake of business, and the best interest of his daughter, he at-tempts to arrange a marriage between Catelina and Spanish Captain Alonso. However, when Ca-talunya signs a treaty with France against Spain, Pau looks north for a suitable husband for his daughter.

After Mateo Amador – Catelina's true love – disappears, Catelina agrees to marry French Captain Louis Bouchard who then begins an attempt to make Catelina French.

Catelina, cut off from her family and desperately unhappy, tries to escape from her hus-band. At the same time, Mateo resurfaces and promises Pau he will find Catelina and bring her home. Eventually, they find each other and go into hiding.

When an agreement between France and Spain to end the thirty-year war cedes North Ca-talunya to France, Mateo and Catalina decide to return to Barcelona. However, their path crosses Bouchard and a pregnant Catelina is injured and dies on November 7, 1659 (symbolising the death/loss of north Catalunya).

The book ends with Bouchard vowing to destroy Mateo who has been the bane of life for too long.

Press Release

Title: Catelina

Author: Judy Rankin

ISBN: 9781784653538

Genre: Historical romance /

Price: £12.99

Imprint: Pegasus

PRESS RELEASE

Pegasus Publishers are pleased to announce the publication of *Catelina*, by Judy Rankin, available to order from bookshops or direct from the publisher

ABOUT THE BOOK
The loyalty of a once-proud nation exploited by a pact it must honour; a war that divides families, friends and communities. Catelina Maria, a stubborn, beautiful and fiercely proud Catalan woman must fight for all she loves and cries out for while the twists of history and fate intervene. Will she keep what her heart holds dear?

And what of her childhood friend, grown into a man who chooses to put his country before all else. Will Mateo Amador lose everything and everyone he values to do his duty for his people?

Can love and duty co-exist, is allegiance more important than family, and must duty ultimately destroy?

Set against the backdrop of the Catalan Revolt during the Franco-Spanish War (1640 - 1659) this vivid tale of danger, honour and love will have you turning the pages until the last one, no matter the time

ABOUT THE AUTHOR
Judy Rankin first appeared on bookshelves in 2014 with the release of the memoir *It's [Not] All About Liz!* Since then, Judy has spent her time teaching English as a second language in various countries in Europe and the UK.

With a home base in Melbourne, Australia, Judy enjoys swapping hats between acting as consultant and mentor for an ESL recruitment company in China, offering editing and ghost-writing services, writing short stories (available on her website www.judyrankin.com) and working on her next novel

CONTACTS
Copies of *Catelina* can be purchased direct from the publisher by visiting our website at www.pegasuspublishers.com or by calling 01223 370012. Contact can be made with the author via the publisher

NEWS

Kids book a family effort

Jaymah

Mission	**Vision**
Jaymah's mission is to support indie writers in publishing their work, gaining exposure, and building their brand.	They say there's safety in numbers. By bringing together indie writers to showcase their work, our vision is to highlight the talent out there being ignored by traditional publishers.

Jaymah is a writing and publishing consultancy operating to support indie writers. Not every story - no matter how compelling - will be published through a traditional publisher. But that doesn't mean the story isn't good enough to be published.

Unfortunately, hybrid publishers aren't always honourable and can be too expensive for an emerging writer. So, at Jaymah, we endeavour to work with writers and allow them to sell their work without having to pay a premium for the privilege.

How do we do this? By creating an arena for writers to join together in one spot (or one site) to sell their books.

All profit from the sale of a book returns to the author.

Jaymah also offers resources for writers who need a little help to get their work formatted and prepared ready for sale. The services offered are charged at a reasonable price and help keep the Jaymah website open and accessible to artists.

About Jaymah's Founder

Judy Rankin Reid - the founder of Jaymah - has a BA (Hons) in Publishing and Professional Writing. She is a published writer, having appeared in *MUFTI*, the Victorian RSL Members' Magazine, *that's life* magazine, several annual anthologies and published novels through traditional and self-publishing. As such, she's been through the lows of endless rejection letters, experienced the highs of seeing her work in print and wants to share her first-hand experiences and knowledge with other writers.

www.ingramcontent.com/pod-product-compliance
Lightning Source LLC
LaVergne TN
LVHW051019080826
845145LV00009B/2696
9780645377088